EARTH'S INNOVATORS

INNOVATORS CHALLENGING CLIMATE CHANGE

Robyn Hardyman

Published in 2020 by
Lucent Press, an Imprint of Greenhaven Publishing, LLC
353 3rd Avenue
Suite 255
New York, NY 10010

Produced for Lucent by Calcium
Designers: Paul Myerscough and Simon Borrough
Picture researcher: Rachel Blount
Editors: Sarah Eason and Jennifer Sanderson

Picture credits: Cover: Shutterstock: Artistic Photo; Inside: 4per1000: pp. 40э, 40b; Calysta: p. 41; Flickr: NASA: p. 4; Goldman Environmental Prize: pp. 9, 16; Graviky Labs: p. 35; Lightyear: pp. 30, 31; Shutterstock: Airphoto.gr: p. 11; Alexander-Glover: p. 21; Anyaivanova: pp. 1r, 37; Malcolm Chapman: pp. 42-43; Hung Chung Chih: pp. 1cl, 32; Rob Crandall: p. 28; Grzegorz Czapski: p. 29; Ermess: p. 24; Joe Ferrer: p. 10; Gestalt Imagery: p. 38; Faina Gurevich: p. 15; Gyuszko-Photo: pp. 3, 19; Jacob_09: pp. 44-45; Joel_420: p. 27; KAMONRAT: p. 17; Krista Kennell: p. 6; Philip Lange: p. 26; Mikhail Leonov: pp. 1l, 39; Dmitri Ma: p. 8; Oleksiy Mark: p. 25; Mykola Mazuryk: p 5; Neil Mitchell: pp. 1cr, 34; MrNovel: p. 14; Robert Nyholm: p. 20; Mikhail Roop: p. 7; CL Shebley: p. 12; Ivan Smuk: p. 18; Wikimedia Commons: ArCaRa: p. 33; Dipl. Ing. Guido Grassow: p. 13; Ministry of Science & Technology (GODL-India (https://data.gov.in/sites/default/files/Gazette_Notification_OGDL.pdf)): p. 36; Planet Labs, Inc.: p. 22; Raysonho @ Open Grid Scheduler / Grid Engine: p. 23.

Cataloging-in-Publication Data

Names: Hardyman, Robyn.
Title: Innovators challenging climate change / Robyn Hardyman.
Description: New York : Lucent Press, 2020. | Series: Earth's innovators | Includes glossary and index.
Identifiers: ISBN 9781534565579 (pbk.) | ISBN 9781534565586 (library bound) | ISBN 9781534565593 (ebook)
Subjects: LCSH: Climatic changes--Juvenile literature. | Global warming--Juvenile literature. | Climatic changes--Prevention--Technological innovations--Juvenile literature. | Climatic changes--Risk management--Juvenile literature. | Global warming--Prevention--Technological innovations--Juvenile literature.
Classification: LCC QC981.8.C5 H37 2020 | DDC 551.6--dc23

Contents

CHAPTER 1

A TRULY GLOBAL CHALLENGE

Climate is the regular pattern of weather in a location over a long period. It is the big picture of how much it rains and whether it is generally cold or warm. The climate is different around the world from place to place, but the global climate is the average climate around the whole world. In recent decades, the global climate has started to change. This global climate change is what scientists are worried about, because it is having a negative effect on our planet.

Getting Hotter

Earth is gradually warming up, and it is happening faster than at any time in the history of the world. The air temperature near Earth's surface rose almost 1.5 degrees Fahrenheit (0.8 degrees C) in the last century. Earth has warmed twice as fast in the last 50 years as in the 50 years before that. Although 1.5 degrees may not seem like a lot, it is enough to cause many damaging changes.

1980   2012

In the Arctic, some of the ice never melts. These two photos show how the amount of ice that remains there through the summer has reduced dramatically since 1980. This is because of global warming.

Climate change is making some areas of the world much drier. Drought makes it impossible for farmers to grow crops.

Scientists have learned that this rise in temperature is because of the way we are living. Our homes, industry, transportation, and agriculture are all emitting gases called greenhouse gases. These are collecting above us in Earth's atmosphere. They act like a blanket around Earth, trapping the heat from the sun so it cannot escape. This warms the overall air temperature around the world.

The worst greenhouse gas is carbon dioxide, or CO_2. This is emitted when we burn fossil fuels such as coal, oil, and natural gas. We do this all the time in power stations to create electricity, which powers just about everything, and in our cars when we drive on gasoline or diesel.

Does It Matter?

Global warming certainly does matter because it is making the climate change. As the world warms, the ice at the North and South Poles is melting. This makes the sea level rise, which is dangerous for people living along coastlines. Millions of people could lose their homes if this continues. Other effects of a warmer world are drought, or long periods without rain, in some areas, and flooding, caused by heavier rainfall, in others. Extremes of weather are becoming much more common as the world is warming.

Climate change is the most serious problem facing the world today, and it is a truly global challenge. It affects both rich and poor countries, and people everywhere are working hard to find solutions.

Getting Prepared

While people are working hard to prevent the causes of climate change from becoming worse, there are some effects that are too late to stop. Governments and individuals are focused on preparing for these, such as extremes of weather and the effects of rising sea levels. This is known as building resilience.

Building Resilience

Climate resilience is the ability to anticipate, prepare for, and respond to hazardous events or disturbances related to the climate. We need to understand how climate change will create risks for us and prepare for those risks. Businesses, for example, are looking at ways to respond to extreme weather events such as storms and floods. Countries and states are bringing people together to work on solutions. In the United States, at least 15 states already have climate resilience plans, and more are developing them. Examples include how to look after communities along the coast that may be threatened by rising sea levels, or communities that are especially likely to experience floods after heavy rainfall.

California has advanced climate resilience plans. Its former governor, Arnold Schwarzenegger, worked hard to start this process.

Wildfires are a common sight in California, causing damage to people's farmland, businesses, and property.

Preparation in California

In the United States, California is leading the way in working to combat climate change. The state is being hit by record droughts and rainfalls, resulting in wildfires, flooding, and mudslides. In 2006, California's governor, Arnold Schwarzenegger, made a new law, the Global Warming Solutions Act, which requires the state to reduce its greenhouse gas emissions to the levels they were at in 1990 by 2020. That goal is on track, and the state is now aiming for a target of 80 percent below 1990 levels by 2050. California's emissions are 40 percent lower than the U.S. average.

Meanwhile, California also has measures for protecting land and property from fire. One of these is building with materials that are less likely to catch fire, so not with wood,

for example. Another is making sure there is space around a property, so that if one house is ablaze, the flames will not automatically spread to the next one. Out in open country, wide strips of vegetation can be cleared, so that a fire will have nothing to burn when it reaches them and it will stop moving forward.

INGENIOUS INNOVATIONS

The latest technology for fighting wildfires uses water in a new way: mist. Spraying a fire with very fine droplets of mist works because these droplets absorb more of the heat from the fire. They can also cover a wider area than gushes of water.

Zero Waste Network

Each day, we throw away an incredible amount of trash, and this adds up into millions of tons of waste. In many developed countries, one way of dealing with this waste has been to burn it. This is done in giant burners called incinerators. The process releases a lot of harmful gases into the atmosphere. In Italy, one man was determined to put a stop to this in his local community.

Rossano Ercolini was an elementary school teacher in a small town in central Italy called Capannori. When a plan was announced for a large incinerator to be built near his town, he began to organize local people to protest. He felt that, as an educator, it was his duty to protect the well-being of the community.

Old waste incinerator plants like this one release harmful gases.

From Educator to Innovator

Local government officials were so impressed with Ercolini's protest that they canceled plans for the incinerator. They put Ercolini in charge of developing a new waste-management plan instead. Ercolini was passionate about recycling, separating out the different types of waste, and sending them to be processed so that they could be reused. Within a year, his new plan was in place and his town was recycling more than 80 percent of its garbage.

That was certainly not the end of it, however. Ercolini's views on reducing the amount of waste we produce, and disposing of it in a sustainable way, caught on even further. Soon his whole province had closed down its incinerators and implemented more recycling. This approach is known as Zero Waste, and Ercolini's pioneering work helped the Zero Waste Network to spread not just through Italy, but across the whole of Europe. Millions of people now recycle their waste and work to produce less of it in the first place.

A Global Movement

Ercolini is now president of Zero Waste Europe, a thriving organization that is changing the way the continent deals with the problem of garbage and more. It works for the reduction of greenhouse gases and air pollution through zero-waste solutions. His remarkable work shows that a single individual really can make big changes happen. Ercolini has been honored with the Goldman Environmental Prize, the highest award given in recognition of work that improves the sustainability of our lives. There is a Zero Waste Network in the United States, working toward the same goals.

Rossano Ercolini believed that an individual could make a difference, and he did.

9

CHAPTER 2

ELECTRICITY

Our need for electricity is one of the biggest factors contributing to the greenhouse gases that are causing climate change. Making the electricity for our homes and businesses produces nearly 30 percent of all the greenhouse gas emissions in the United States. This is because, traditionally, we have made electricity by burning fossil fuels, such as coal, oil, and natural gas. When burned, these produce high levels of greenhouse gases. Innovators are working on new ways to produce electricity that are cleaner and kinder to our planet.

Working Together

A challenge on this scale needs inspired individuals, researchers, businesses, and governments to work together. In one innovative city in the United States, people are doing just that. The city of Minneapolis, in Minnesota, decided it would set a target to reduce its greenhouse gas emissions by 80 percent by the year 2050. It soon became clear, however, that the goal could not be met without substantial help from the area's two electricity and gas companies, Xcel Energy and CenterPoint Energy. Together they formed the Minneapolis Clean Energy Partnership (CEP).

Electric trains run through the central business district of Minneapolis.

Power plants that burn coal or oil to produce electricity produce high levels of greenhouse gases.

The mayor, city councillors, city coordinators, and senior representatives from the two energy companies regularly meet to plan policies that will promote clean energy activity across the city. Steps the partnership has taken include encouraging commercial property owners, landlords, and individual homeowners to conserve energy—as well as continuing efforts to cut the electricity and gas usage of city-owned buildings, streetlights, and vehicles.

An Inspiring Example

The CEP has drawn national attention. It won a Climate Leadership Award from the U.S. Environmental Protection Agency (EPA). The Department of Energy (DOE) recognized its software program, which helps building owners understand their energy use. Several other U.S. cities have looked to Minneapolis as a model for their own emissions-cutting efforts.

Developing Countries

The rapid economic development in Asia, Latin America, and Africa is an important part of the energy problem. In the past, energy consumption in developing countries has been lower than in the developed world, but as these economies grow and people expect a higher standard of living, their energy use significantly increases. Many of these regions have hot climates, and scientists think the demand for energy for cooling is soon going to be an even greater challenge than for heating. Innovative solutions are coming out of these regions, too.

Clean Energy

The solution to our problem of greenhouse gases lies in using cleaner sources to create electricity that produce zero emissions. Fortunately, these sources are all around us and they are plentiful. These are the renewable energy sources such as sunlight, the wind, the oceans, and the heat in the ground.

All around the world, people are creating small-scale projects in their local communities, they are pushing the boundaries of our knowledge in research labs, and they are working hard to influence governments and big business. Already about one-fifth of the world's energy comes from renewable sources, but there is still a long way to go.

Solar Power

Solar power is the world's fastest-growing source of energy. Recent years have seen incredible innovations in making it more efficient, more flexible in its uses, and much cheaper. Sunlight is turned into electricity using solar panels, in a process called photovoltaics, or PV. These panels are made using thin wafers of silicon, which absorb the energy in sunlight and turn it into an electric current. Solar power can be generated on a large scale at a solar-power farm, or on a small scale on a single rooftop.

Solar panels on the roof provide this house's residents with electricity, with no harmful emissions.

These floating structures are creating electricity from the movement of the water. They are being tested at a port in Portugal.

INGENIOUS INNOVATIONS

In many cities, the water supply is a large consumer of energy. In Washington, D.C., DC Water treats waste water and provides drinking water for more than 2 million people in the city and four of its surrounding counties. It uses a new technology to create a biogas from the waste in the water. Biogas is any gas made using a product derived from living things. This clean fuel is then used to power the treatment process, in an environmentally friendly cycle.

Wind Power

The wind is always blowing and that movement is a type of energy. To make electricity from the wind, we use its movement to turn the blades of wind turbines. The blades are connected to a machine that generates electricity, which can then be stored. One wind turbine will not create much electricity, so the turbines are usually grouped together in wind farms. These may be on the land in windy places or out at sea, where the wind is stronger. Innovators in wind power are looking at the designs of turbines to make them more efficient. They are even mounting turbines on huge "kites," which glide through the air to "collect" the wind.

Land and Ocean

Other clean energy sources include wave power, which harnesses the movement in the ocean swell, and geothermal energy. Geothermal energy is the heat that lies naturally underground. We can use it to heat water, which makes steam to generate electricity.

Small Is Beautiful

In the developed world, we mainly get our electricity from the big utility companies. We sign up with them and know we can have power in our homes at the flick of a switch. This is possible because of the grid, the network of power stations and cables across the country that reaches to almost every building. In developing countries, however, the grid does not reach nearly as far. Many areas cannot rely on access to electricity. Innovations in energy supply are making a big difference in these communities.

Making a Difference

In Côte d'Ivoire in West Africa, Ghislain Dessieh founded Africa For Green. Many people in rural areas of his country cook their food on open fires, using wood as fuel. This creates a lot of harmful smoke. Dessieh has developed a kit that households can use to make

In this community of shacks on the outskirts of a city in South Africa, the only source of electricity is a solar panel mounted on the roof.

In Denver, Colorado, solar panels above the tables of a street cafe provide electricity to the business.

biogas from their own household waste. They can use this gas for cooking, in a much cleaner, less-polluting way. Also in West Africa, in Mali, Cherif Haidara is making solar-powered lamps with local materials, to bring clean energy to remote areas of his country. This means that children can do their schoolwork, and people can work and go out safely after dark.

On the other side of the African continent, in Kenya, another innovator, Tony Niagah, is working on a solar-powered tile that can be installed on people's roofs to give them electricity, even if they are not on the grid. Also in Kenya, Evans Wadongo founded GreenWize Energy, a support organization to advance the development of all kinds of innovative green energy products in Africa.

Power Sharing

Not all homes can use solar panels, however, especially in the developed world, where people live mostly in densely built cities. People living in apartment blocks, for example, may not have access to a rooftop. One young energy innovator in Colorado had an idea to solve this problem. David Amster-Olszewski started a business called SunShare. SunShare builds "gardens" of solar panels on available land in a community and invites local residents to buy a share in those panels. Residents who have bought into the project receive credits on their utility bill, based on how much electricity their solar panels produce. The idea caught on quickly and, today, nearly 100 community solar projects are operating in different states across the United States.

Khanh Nguy Thi

Vietnam is a country in Southeast Asia that has a booming economy. As a result, its need for electricity to power all its factories, businesses, and homes has grown fast. When the question of how all the electricity should be generated was being discussed, one woman stepped forward to encourage the government to make sustainable, environmentally friendly choices. She is Khanh Nguy Thi.

Khanh Nguy Thi had no background or expertise in energy. She grew up in a small village in Vietnam and studied history in college, but she had always cared about the environment. Her village was near a coal-fired power station, so she saw firsthand the pollution and the dust it caused. The dust even made some local people develop diseases. Coal-fired power stations are the dirtiest way to generate power. Nguy Thi saw that her country was at a critical point in its growth, and that this was the time to make better choices for its people and for the planet.

Khan Nguy Thi won the Goldman Environmental Prize for her pioneering work in changing the government's energy policy in Vietnam.

Time to Act

When the Vietnamese government published plans to build more coal-fired power stations, Nguy Thi felt she must act. A study by scientists at Harvard University in Massachusetts concluded that about 20,000 people a year could die in Vietnam as a result of the air pollution. Nguy Thi set up the Vietnam Sustainable Energy Alliance, a network of 11 Vietnamese and international environmental and social organizations that work together on energy issues. She brought them together to influence the country's decision makers.

Determination and Leadership

Nguy Thi taught herself all about coal and climate change, and persuaded others that it was time for change. She worked with energy experts to develop a different energy plan for Vietnam that she could present to her government. She also worked with the media to publish evidence about the harm caused by coal. When there were several coal-related environmental disasters in Vietnam, the topic caught the public's attention.

Nguy Thi's amazing determination led to an extraordinary result. In 2016, the Vietnamese government announced it was changing its energy plan. It significantly reduced the number of coal plants, and included Nguy Thi's recommendation to increase renewable energy, such as wind and solar, to 21 percent of the total energy plan by 2030. One single individual has made a real difference. In 2018, Nguy Thi was honored with the prestigious Goldman Environmental Prize for her remarkable work.

17

CHAPTER 3

BUILDINGS

Many of our buildings were constructed before people thought very carefully about how they use energy. We heat our homes with expensive electricity, then we let a lot of that heat escape through the windows, roof, and walls. If we could make sure that our buildings kept the heat inside more effectively, we would need to use less energy to stay warm. Innovators are also looking at ways to make buildings generate their own electricity.

Collaboration

In Europe, 12 partners in universities, research, and industry are working together on a project called ISOBIO. This project is aiming to deliver better materials for constructing and insulating buildings. It is working on bio-based insulation, which is insulating materials that use products from plants and animals. That could include using animal wool or straw, for example.
One business in France has produced an insulation panel that is made from the hemp plant. These products work just as well as traditional ones, which often use plastics or fiberglass, but they improve the energy efficiency of buildings in a greener way.

A special camera shows the temperature of the outside surfaces of these houses. The orange and red areas are losing a lot of heat because of lack of insulation in the walls.

24.2

3.1

Leading the Way

Some businesses are leading the way with this innovative technology. Nike, for example, has its European Logistics Campus in Belgium. This environmentally friendly building uses 100 percent renewable sources for its energy needs, including solar, wind, and water power. The lights switch on and off as staff move around, and 95 percent of the building's waste is recycled. Many staff cycle to work or arrive by boat on the canal that runs alongside the campus. There are even bees and sheep in the green areas outside.

Freiburg in Germany is aiming to be one of the greenest cities in the world. The new houses there are designed to need very little energy for heating or cooling, and their electricity comes from solar power.

Cooling

In many parts of the world, everyday temperatures mean that buildings need cooling, rather than heating. These are often countries where the economy is growing fast, and many more people can afford to cool their homes. In fact, the experts estimate that the growing need for cooling in hot countries is likely to be a bigger contributor to climate change than the world's need for heating. We need to find more environmentally friendly ways to keep places cool. One Korean company, LG, has created a solar-assisted air conditioner, and in the United States, Lennox has developed the SunSource, which can power either heating or cooling.

In this pioneering new solar village in Freiberg, all the houses use clean and renewable energy sources.

Local Power

One of the advantages of renewable energy systems is that they can be located exactly where they are needed. The energy is generated on-site, and stored in a battery, ready to power the devices inside the building. These innovations are bringing energy generation close to home, and are certain to be incorporated in the buildings of the future.

Roof Power

It is amazing how much of the electricity demand in the United States could be supplied by rooftop solar panels. In 2018, the National Renewable Energy Laboratory (NREL) released a report on the subject. The report found that of the 116.9 million residential buildings in the United States, 67.2 million of them are suitable for solar panels—that is more than half. If they all had solar panels installed, about 75 percent of all the energy consumed in homes could be provided this way. That electricity would be generated with zero emissions, so it would make a huge contribution to reducing the country's production of greenhouse gases.

This house gets its hot water from these solar water heaters on the roof.

Hot Water

Solar power can be used not just to generate electricity, but also to provide hot water for showers and laundry. A solar water heater on the roof collects the sun's heat using a device called a collector. It heats water that is then pumped to a storage tank. The first collectors were not very efficient at heating the water, but the latest innovation, called the evacuated tube collector, does a much better job. It consists of a series of metal pipes containing a liquid that heats up. Each pipe is enclosed in a double-walled glass tube, painted black to absorb more heat. Solar water heaters are ideal for sunny areas.

INGENIOUS INNOVATIONS

Peter Brook is an architect in Australia who wanted to be able to solar power a skyscraper. To generate enough energy for such a large building, an enormous area of panels is needed. The roof could never be big enough. However, when more flexible panels were developed, he thought of putting them not on the roof, but on the walls of his building. His Sol Invictus tower in Melbourne is a 60-story building with solar panels wrapped around its outside. Once it is complete, solar power will provide half of the building's energy needs.

This office block in Manchester, United Kingdom (U.K.), is covered in solar panels that provide a significant amount of its electricity. It is one of the U.K.'s most energy-efficient buildings.

Tesla

Tesla is a U.S. company that makes electric cars. It is an innovator and world leader in that technology, working hard to develop batteries that can store more power, so that electric cars can be driven for more miles before they need to be recharged. Tesla is breaking new ground in other ways, too, in its incredible new building and its solar-power products.

Tesla hopes to be producing 500,000 electric cars a year in the near future. To enable the company to do this, it needs a very big factory, a Gigafactory, in fact. Work began on this building outside Sparks, Nevada, in 2014, and by the time it is finished, Tesla expects it to be the biggest building in the world. What is even more remarkable is that the company plans for it to be powered entirely by renewable energy, mainly solar.

The Tesla Gigafactory is under construction and, when complete, will be the biggest building in the world.

Building a Giant Factory

By late 2018, the Gigafactory was about one-third complete, and parts of it were already in use, building electric motors and battery packs. It already had a footprint of more than 1.9 million square feet (176,500 sq m) and a working space of 4.9 million square feet (455,200 sq m) on several floors. This record-breaking building is scheduled for completion in 2020.

A Renewable World

Tesla is a genuine innovator, and on a huge scale. As well as making electric cars and their batteries, the company wants to do all it can to accelerate the world's transition to renewable energy. To generate that energy, it has developed solar roof tiles. These are shaped like regular roof tiles, but they are actually PV panels. There are four different styles to choose from, to suit the style of the building. Made with glass, they are more than three times stronger than standard roofing tiles and can withstand even the most violent hailstorm, wind, or fire.

To store the energy that the solar roof tiles create, Tesla is manufacturing a large battery for the home, called the Powerwall. During the day when the sun shines, the roof tiles generate electricity. Any that is not used immediately is fed into the Powerwall. It is then ready for use after dark, or whenever you need it. Tesla's innovative and ambitious vision of the self-powered home is an important part of tackling the challenge of climate change.

For larger houses, users can install additional Powerwalls to power more of the electrical devices around the house.

CHAPTER 4

TRANSPORTATION

Transportation is the largest source of greenhouse gas emissions in the United States. We just love our cars, trucks, and airplanes, but unfortunately, the planet does not. Burning diesel, gasoline, and aviation fuel produces huge amounts of greenhouse gases that are contributing to global warming and climate change. We need to find innovative ways to stop this pollution, without bringing our transportation to a stop.

There are many innovative ways to tackle this challenge. Some are on a big scale, like redesigning our city transportation networks, or finding new fuels to power our vehicles. Others are on a very small scale, like individuals choosing to take fewer car journeys.

This electric-diesel vehicle is competing in the Shell Eco Marathon.

Tackling Fuel

The first area to tackle is fuel. Our engines are designed to run on gasoline and diesel, but there is work being done to make these more efficient, so that they deliver more miles for fewer gallons. A combination of engine design, vehicle design, and fuel design is producing good results. Every year at the Eco Marathon, which the giant oil company Shell runs, teams of people compete with their specially designed cars to travel the farthest on the least amount of fuel.

Diesel and gasoline can be made cleaner by being blended with biofuels. These are fuels made from plants. Not only are they cleaner, but they are also renewable. New biofuels are being developed all the time, but the main ones currently in use are made from corn or sugar cane. Biofuel made from sugarcane has 70 percent fewer emissions than gasoline.

The thousands of trucks that thunder along our highways spew out dirty emissions at an alarming rate. Innovators are developing a new fuel for their engines, too. Called liquid natural gas (LNG), this is still a fossil fuel, but it produces much fewer harmful gases.

Refueling Problems

Of course vehicles need fueling stations, and people will be reluctant to use new fuels if they are not easily available. Shell is developing a network of LNG fuel stations in the United States, starting in Texas, Louisiana, and California. There are already hundreds of biodiesel fueling stations across the country, as well as in Europe.

Vast railroad networks can be used to transport liquid biofuels to where they are needed.

Electric Vehicles

The best way to reduce the pollution from our vehicles would be to remove their engines altogether. In the last decade there have been amazing advances in the technology of electric cars. Instead of an engine, these have an electric motor. The electricity to power the motor comes from a large battery. The challenge is to make a battery that can store enough electricity to power the car for a long drive. Drivers ideally need to be able to drive for several hundred miles on a single charge.

Clean Cities

Tesla is pioneering the development of better batteries. So far, the company's best battery can drive around 300 miles (480 km) before needing to be recharged. Innovators are developing batteries for buses and trucks, too. These have space for a much bigger battery to power the vehicle for more miles. Cities around the world are introducing electric buses to improve the air quality in their city centers and to encourage more people to use public transportation. Some have plans to make these areas zero-emission zones over the next five to ten years. This will mean that all standard engines will be banned.

Unlike diesel-powered buses, electric buses do not pollute the city streets.

The Nissan Leaf can be charged at an on-street charging station in around 30 minutes.

Where to Recharge

One challenge in introducing more electric vehicles is having enough places to recharge them. There is a good network of charging points across the United States but other countries are behind. It takes several hours to recharge a battery fully at a standard household electric outlet, so many people with electric cars charge them overnight at home. There is a new way to do this, however, which is much quicker. At a special charging station, using a higher voltage supply, they can get more electricity into the battery quickly. This can provide an 80 percent charge in around 30 minutes, but that is still a long time to wait. If the charging station is in a parking lot, drivers can park and leave their vehicle there while they go to work or go shopping. Charging the car at a station costs money, but to encourage drivers to switch to electric cars, some governments are offering drivers some of that money back through a variety of schemes.

Although electric cars are a great, cleaner alternative to gasoline-run vehicles, they still consume a lot of energy. This is because the electricity they run on has to be produced somehow. If it is made at a coal-powered power plant, it is still polluting the atmosphere and adding to the problem of climate change.

Hydrogen

There is an alternative to standard electric cars that is totally clean. The only waste product from using it to power a car is water—there are no harmful emissions at all. This is hydrogen, a gas that is one of the most plentiful substances on the planet. Innovations in hydrogen-powered vehicles are some of the most exciting in transportation today.

Fuel Cells

Unlike with standard fuels, hydrogen is not burned in a car's engine. It is used in a device, called a fuel cell, inside the car to make electricity, which is then used to power an electric motor that drives the vehicle. Inside the fuel cell, hydrogen is combined with oxygen and, in the process, it makes water and electricity. So the fuel cell is a bit like a battery that can never run flat, as long as there is a supply of hydrogen in the tank. A single tank can take a car for several hundred miles. This makes hydrogen cars more attractive than standard electric cars with a limited range. You can also refill the tank with hydrogen in a couple of minutes, instead of waiting hours for a battery to recharge.

In the not-too-distant future, we may see far more of these hydrogen fuel pumps in our fueling stations.

Companies Leading the Way

There are several hydrogen-powered cars on the road, such as the Honda Clarity and the Toyota Mirai. Toyota, Daimler, and BMW are leading a group of 13 companies around the world, investing $10 billion over the next 10 years in developing hydrogen technology and supply systems.

The countries leading the way in hydrogen vehicles are the United States, Germany, and Japan. California leads the way in the United States, with more hydrogen stations than any other state, but there is still a long way to go.

In 2018, Hyundai showed its Nexo, which is powered by a hydrogen fuel cell. It has a driving range of around 500 miles (800 km).

INGENIOUS INNOVATIONS

Swindon is a small town in the south of the U.K. that is leading the way in developing hydrogen technology for that country. The U.K.'s first fully renewable hydrogen station opened in a Honda dealership there. Because there is no network of hydrogen supply in the U.K. yet, Honda designed an innovative solution, which was to produce their own hydrogen, on a commercial scale, using solar power. This hydrogen supply now serves the world's first hybrid vans, which run on a mix of sustainable biodiesel and hydrogen, and the U.K.'s first hydrogen-powered forklift trucks. There is also a hydrogen-powered Education Center on the site.

Lightyear

It all started with five friends who were studying at the University of Technology in Eindhoven in the Netherlands. Lex Hoefsloot, Arjo van der Ham, Martijn Lammers, Qurein Biewenga, and Koen van Ham were all passionate about finding solutions to the problem of global warming and climate change.

The friends believed it could be possible to create an electric car that was powered by the sun. They knew that every year in the Solar Challenge, teams from around the world competed to design and race their solar-powered cars, and they were determined to enter. They built a car called Stella and, in 2012, entered the race. Competing against 45 teams, Stella won, driving from north to south through Australia. This car could drive at 40 miles per hour (65 km/h) and generate more electricity than it was using. The friends were delighted, and knew they were onto something big. They improved Stella and won the challenge for a second and then a third time. That is where the idea to build a family solar car was sparked.

The Lightyear team has a passion for finding cleaner ways to power our transportation.

> The Lightyear One is lightweight, to use less energy, and each wheel has its own motor, which reduces the number of moving parts and thus the need for maintenance.

Making It Happen

The friends set up a business called Lightyear. When they began looking for support, they found that a lot of people in the automotive industry were looking for a project that could really impact the world. They hired skilled business people to add to their technological expertise. Then, they set about developing their car—the Lightyear One.

Sun Power

The Lightyear One is a car that charges itself with sunlight, through solar cells that are built into its roof. This way of powering a car greatly reduces dependency on the electricity grid. It is not yet possible to charge a car completely with solar power, but as long as the Lightyear One is in a reasonably sunny place, the solar cells can provide more than 40 percent of its power. The more sunshine it has, the more power it can generate. When the car does need an electricity supplement, this can come from a standard power socket, found anywhere. People can start driving this car, anywhere in the world, without needing to wait for the recharging network to improve.

The team at Lightyear says it feels a big sense of obligation to develop the car because, together, its members know they have the skills and the technology to solve one of the world's really big problems. They believe that solar cars will play a large part in making us switch to electric cars. In 2018, Lightyear won a Climate Change Innovator Award in Los Angeles, California, and the company has attracted the funding it needs to take the Lightyear One to the next stage.

CHAPTER 5

INDUSTRY

Along with transportation, one of the biggest contributors to global warming and climate change is industry, especially heavy industry, such as plants manufacturing chemicals and steel, for example. These huge plants spew harmful emissions into the atmosphere. Fortunately, governments around the world recognize this problem, and innovations are underway to clean up their operations.

Growth in China

This problem is often worst in low- and middle-income countries, where many new industries grow quickly. There are often fewer controls on emission levels and air quality. The economy of China has grown massively over the last 20 years. The country has seen rapid industrialization but with all those new factories, comes more pollution. In China, more than 1 million people are thought to die every year from air pollution. The pollution comes from a mix of emissions from transportation, coal-fired power plants, and heavy industry. Now, however, the country is fighting back with innovative solutions.

Air pollution is damaging the health of many children in the worst-affected cities in China.

Special tiles on the outside of the Torre de Especialidades hospital in Mexico City help take pollutants out of the air.

Change in China

As well as investing heavily in renewable energy such as solar and wind, and closing coal-fired power plants, the Chinese government is taking steps to reduce the pollution from industry. It is reducing the amount of steel it makes. It has also introduced strict new rules on air quality, which it is trying to enforce. It has built a nationwide network of monitors tracking the levels of harmful particles in the air. The data from all these monitors is publicly available, so that anyone with a cell phone can now check their local air quality in real time. They can also report pollutors to local enforcement agencies using social media.

Buildings

Architects have been looking at ways to design buildings that clean dirty air. It turns out that relatively straightforward chemical reactions to improve air quality can be triggered with a little help from the sun. In Mexico City, Mexico, where air pollution is a serious problem, a hospital building called the Torre de Especialidades has a front made of special tiles. These are coated with a substance called titanium dioxide. When sunlight hits them, harmful pollutants in the air are turned into less-harmful substances. Other innovators have developed a type of concrete that does the same thing. It could be used in buildings around the world to clean our air.

33

Carbon Capture

Power and industry produce about 50 percent of all greenhouse gas emissions worldwide. Experts say that there are two main ways to deal with the problem: to reduce the levels of emissions, and to make the emissions less harmful. For example, the most effective way to make carbon dioxide less harmful is to take the carbon out of it. This is called carbon capture.

There are three parts to the carbon-capture process: capturing the carbon dioxide, transporting it by pipeline or ship, and either securely storing it or using it for another purpose. The carbon dioxide is stored underground, in empty oil and gas fields, or in other rock formations several miles below Earth's surface. The International Energy Agency (IEA) states that carbon capture could reduce our global carbon dioxide emissions by 19 percent.

Drax Power Station in the U.K. sends clouds of smoke and steam into the atmosphere today, but it has plans to capture the carbon it produces instead.

Global Innovation

Today, there are 22 carbon capture projects in operation in the world, and there are plans to increase this number. The Carbon Capture Innovation Challenge is an international effort to find and support breakthrough technologies in this area. Countries around the world are working together on this. In May 2018, for example, the U.K. government announced it would lead an international challenge with Saudi Arabia and Mexico to support a new technology that would make carbon capture more affordable. Drax Power Station in the U.K. is set to become the largest decarbonization project in Europe.

INGENIOUS INNOVATIONS

Large-scale carbon-capture innovation requires the cooperation and funding of governments, but one Indian innovator has found a small-scale solution. Anirudh Sharma has found a way to harvest the black smoke from chimneys and car exhausts and turn it into ink. The smoke contains unburned carbon. This is collected and cleaned, then mixed with alcohol and oil. The result is a cheaper alternative to traditional ink. Called Kaalink, the project started as a research experiment at Massachusetts Institute of Technology (MIT), where Sharma studied.

Now, he and his team at Sbalabs, a spinoff of the MIT Media Lab, are hoping to partner with companies to take their product worldwide. Small devices will be attached to cars to capture the carbon. For every 6 miles (10 km) the car travels, enough carbon is produced to generate two cartridges of ink.

Air-Ink is ink made from waste carbon.

Mission Innovation

The global community has made remarkable progress in reducing the costs and increasing the use of key clean energy options. However, this is still not enough to meet our long-term climate goals, while providing affordable, reliable, and secure energy. The power of innovation can push down costs and bring new ideas into the mix. In Europe, an organization called Mission Innovation has been set up to help this happen.

Global Innovation

Mission Innovation is a collaboration between 23 countries and the European Union (EU). Member countries outside the EU include the United States, Canada, Mexico, Brazil, China, India, Saudi Arabia, South Korea, Japan, and Australia. Mission Innovation was launched in 2015, and these countries are taking action to double their investment in clean energy by 2020. Their members share information, and work with businesses and investors to develop their goals. This is innovation on a big scale, a truly global effort.

The second Mission Innovation meeting was held in Beijing, China, in 2017. Energy ministers and other high-level delegates from the 24 member countries met to discuss clean energy policies and actions.

Setting Challenges

Mission Innovation has drawn up eight Innovation Challenges, or priorities, for member countries to focus on when supporting research and development. These are:

1 Smart grids: electricity grids powered by renewable sources
2 Off-grid access: ways for communities not on the grid to access electricity from renewable energy sources
3 Carbon capture: innovation to remove harmful carbon dioxide emissions from power plants and industries
4 Biofuels: advancing cleaner fuels for transportation and industry
5 Solar power: developing cheaper and more efficient ways to make electricity from sunlight
6 Clean energy: developing other high-performance clean energy processes
7 Affordable heating and cooling: making clean heating and cooling affordable for everyone
8 Hydrogen: developing the production, storage, and use of hydrogen as an energy solution

Solar power farms like this one can provide clean electricity to thousands of homes and businesses.

Great Progress

In carbon capture and storage, the leading nations are the U.K., Mexico, and Saudi Arabia. In sustainable biofuels, they are Canada, Brazil, China, and India. Each challenge launch calls for research proposals, holds workshops with experts, and invites businesses to invest their money in the best projects. The members of Mission Innovation come together each year at a Mission Innovation Ministerial. At the 2018 event in Sweden, it was announced that an additional $4 billion of government money has so far been invested in clean energy innovation, and nearly 40 new international research and innovation partnerships have been started. A new Champions program was launched to find and to recognize outstanding individuals making real change happen.

CHAPTER 6

AGRICULTURE AND LAND USE

With the world's population at more than 7 billion and growing, there is an ever-increasing need for food. In the last few decades, wealthy countries have developed their agriculture in ways that have enabled them to produce a lot of food, relatively cheaply. Agriculture is very big business. The problem is that agriculture on this scale is contributing to climate change.

Experts say food production is responsible for about 14 percent of greenhouse gas emissions. Broader land-use decisions have an even greater impact. We need to change the ways we grow food and manage the land to be kinder to the environment. As the world warms and the climate changes, agriculture is also one of the first businesses to suffer.

Methane

Farming livestock, such as cattle, releases significant amounts of methane, a powerful greenhouse gas, into the atmosphere. During digestion, cattle create methane and this is released via their belches. Capturing methane and removing it from the atmosphere

Western cattle each release about 265 pounds (120 kg) of methane into the atmosphere per year. In comparison, a sheep releases 18 pounds (8 kg), and a chicken 0.03 pound (0.015 kg).

Growing grain crops on large commercial farms uses a lot of fertilizers that pollute the planet. Many of the crops are grown to feed the cattle that are also big pollutors.

is more difficult than capturing carbon, but scientists are working on innovative ways to do this. For example, they have found a type of bacteria that digests methane. One of the products of that process is a chemical that can be used in manufacturing hydrogen fuel. Chemists are looking at ways of reproducing this process artificially.

More Carbon Dioxide

Another way in which farming livestock contributes to climate change is that the animals are fed on crops that use an enormous amount of land to grow. When grassland is plowed and sowed with cereal crops to feed livestock, that grass is lost. The grass had been absorbing a lot of carbon dioxide from the atmosphere, but that capacity has now gone.

Nitrous Oxide

Another greenhouse gas produced by agriculture is nitrous oxide. This comes from the fertilizers that farmers use on their land to improve the quality of their crops. It is used on the crops we eat, and on the crops that feed cattle. The best solution to this problem is to use much less fertilizer. Scientists are developing varieties of crop that will grow well, without the need for massive amounts of fertilizer.

An obvious answer to this problem is to produce and eat less meat and dairy products. We can all help with this. Experts have said that, if the United States reduced its meat consumption by 50 percent, the effect on the environment would be the same as taking 26 million cars off the road.

Carbon Sinks

When farmers plow the land and use it to grow crops, they are reducing the planet's ability to absorb carbon dioxide. When forests are cut down, or grasslands converted, these valuable "carbon sinks" are lost forever. A carbon sink is a natural or man-made system that absorbs carbon dioxide. Innovators today are looking at replacing these carbon sinks, so that they can help in the race to stop global warming.

Brilliant Plants

Why are plants such good carbon sinks? The reason is that they take in carbon dioxide and give out oxygen. This is the opposite of humans: We breathe in oxygen and breathe out carbon dioxide. Plants use the carbon to build their roots and leaves. In the process, they deposit carbon in the ground. Some innovative farmers are now looking at "carbon farming." One project, which is led by France, is called the 4 per 1000 initiative. It aims to increase the amount of carbon in the soil by 0.4 percent per year, through farming practices such as growing trees and crops together, not plowing before sowing new crops, and keeping bare farmland covered. If these practices are used widely enough, they could have a big impact. Soil with more carbon in it is also more fertile, so less fertilizer would be needed.

4 PER 1000

SOILS FOR FOOD SECURITY AND CLIMATE

> **Every year, one-third of the carbon dioxide the world produces is absorbed by plants. The 4 per 1000 initiative aims to increase this by just 0.4 percent.**

Calysta, the company run by Alan Shaw, is turning methane into food for farmed fish and livestock, and for pets.

Working with Farmers

Across the United States, initiatives are growing to promote carbon farming. Some states are giving tax credits to farmers who increase their soil carbon, and many are working to educate farmers about its benefits. Yet again, California leads the way. Nearly half its 58 counties have farmers and ranchers at various stages of developing and implementing carbon-farming plans. California's Healthy Soils Initiative enlists agriculture in the fight against climate change. Carbon farmers can receive money from the state for a variety of soil-improving practices.

INGENIOUS INNOVATIONS

A team of scientists near San Francisco, California, is working to turn methane gas into fish food. At the biotechnology company Calysta, methane gas is pumped into tanks filled with special bacteria. The bacteria digest the methane, turning it into a pure, high-protein ingredient for fish and pet foods. Using waste methane from livestock to make a feed for livestock could one day be such a neat solution!

Biodome

Farming produces a lot of waste. One young engineering student in Morocco was very aware of the problem that agricultural waste presents, and was determined to work on finding a solution. She is Fatima Zahra Beraich.

Energy from Waste

Beraich's idea was to find a way to make use of farm waste, including manure and plant material, and prevent methane from escaping into the atmosphere. Her solution is a process that takes farm waste and uses it to make biogas and compost.

Beriach wanted to work with small farmers in Morocco, to help them use their waste to make their farms more productive and profitable. She founded a company called Biodome, and invited small farmers to become members of a group. The waste from their farms is treated with bacteria, which helps break down the waste. The process produces methane, but collects it securely. The gas is then used by the farmers as an energy source to power their operations. The other product of the process is a solid compost material. This, too, returns to the farms, to fertilize their land.

Any excess compost is sold to other farmers. The beauty of this system lies in its simplicity. Waste from a farm is used to make gas to power the farm and fertilizer to grow more crops, and all without harmful emissions. It saves the farmer money, and helps save the planet, too.

Rich Rewards

Beraich has been widely recognized for her excellent and innovative work. In 2016, the 22nd United Nations Conference on Climate Change was held in Marrakech, Morocco. At the conference, the World Alliance for Clean Technologies was launched. Its aim is to advance the cause of clean technologies by bringing together innovators from around the world to share their experience and develop solutions to propose to governments, corporations, and institutions. Also at the conference, Fatima Zahra Beraich was awarded the prize of Best Woman Entrepreneur.

In Morocco, the Tamayuz Prize is an annual prize given to a person or an institution that has helped improve the lives of women in that country. In 2018, the prime minister of Morocco awarded this prize to Beraich, in recognition of the impact that her work has on the lives of women in small farming communities.

The work of Biodome with small farmers in Morocco saves the farmers money and uses clean energy to power their operations.

INNOVATORS OF THE FUTURE

Around the world, people have woken up to the threat we face from global warming and climate change. We can see its impact already in more extreme weather events, such as droughts and floods. Environmental campaigners are working to spread the message that we need to act now, and scientists are trying to find solutions that will protect our planet for the future.

Sand on Ice

In the Arctic, the sea ice is shrinking as the world warms. One idea for preventing this is being trialed on a lake in northern Alaska. In a project called Ice911, sand is being sprinkled across the surface of the frozen lake to see if it will stop it melting or at least slow the process. White ice reflects sunlight, and its heat, off its surface. Thin ice is less white, so it reflects less light and heat. In fact, it absorbs the heat, and melts. The sand particles sprinkled over the ice are shiny, so the hope is they will reflect more sunlight. If the sand is sprinkled over an area in the Arctic, it may be possible to rebuild the ice.

Clean the Skies

Other projects are looking at solutions in the sky, such as using 16 trillion miniature robots to deflect the sun's heat away from Earth. David Keith, a Harvard scientist, plans to launch a "StratoCruiser" above the Arizona desert, a high-altitude balloon that will spray chemicals into the atmosphere to deflect sunlight and encourage the formation of clouds. However, these projects aiming to influence the planet's climate are untested, and they may have unintended harmful consequences.

On the Ground

We also need to reduce our emissions, rather than try to destroy them after they have already reached the atmosphere. Back on the ground, engineers in Tucson, Arizona, are working on the Solar Bullet. This is a solar-powered train that would carry passengers at 220 miles per hour (354 km/h) the 116 miles (187 km) from Tucson to Phoenix, in just half an hour.

In the Ocean

The global economy needs trade, but current cargo ships are expensive and bad for the environment because they are made of steel. Making steel produces masses of greenhouse gases. The EU is making recyclable ships made from fiber instead of steel.

There are many innovative ideas like these. Around the world, scientists, entrepreneurs, innovators, and leaders are using their STEM (science, technology, engineering, and math) skills to find solutions to the problem of climate change.

It is up to each one of us to live our life in ways that protect our planet for the future.

Glossary

atmosphere the blanket of gases around Earth

bacteria tiny living things

battery a container in which energy is stored, then converted to electricity when needed

biofuels fuels made from living things, such as plants, which are renewable sources

biogas a gas made from natural waste

carbon sinks natural or man-made systems that suck up carbon dioxide from the atmosphere

cleaner creating less pollution

climate change the changes in world climate caused by the increase in air temperature

commercial describes a product or service that is made to be sold to the public

conserve avoid wasteful use

developed countries wealthy countries where most people have good living conditions

developing countries poorer countries that are trying to improve people's living conditions

diesel a liquid fuel, heavier than gasoline

drought a long period without rain

economic relating to money and trade

emissions the release of something into the environment, particularly of pollution

entrepreneur a person who has an idea and starts a new business to develop it

fossil fuels energy sources, such as coal and oil, which formed in the ground over millions of years from the remains of living things

geothermal the heat beneath Earth's surface

green kind to the environment

greenhouse gases gases that trap the heat of the sun in Earth's atmosphere

hybrid using both electricity and diesel or gas

hydrogen a gas found in air and water

income money earned

industrialization the process of growing the industry, such as factories, in a country

insulating keeping in the heat

livestock animals kept for farming, such as cows

logistics the transporting of goods

methane a greenhouse gas produced by cattle during the digestion of plants

motor a machine that converts electrical energy into mechanical energy

photovoltaics (PV) the process of creating electricity from the light of the sun

protein a substance that all animals need to grow and be healthy

renewable sources that do not run out, such as light from the sun, wind, and plants

social concerned with society and people

software program instructions for a computer

solar relating to the sun

sustainable able to continue at the current rate; or a source for making electricity that will never run out, such as the sun or wind

turbines wheels used to convert the movement of air or a liquid into electricity

utility a resource such as electricity, gas, or water provided to homes and businesses

voltage an electric force measured in volts

For More Information

Books

Coutts, Lyn. *Global Warming*. Hauppauge, NY: Barrons Educational Series, 2017.

Sneideman, Joshua ,and Erin Twamley. *Renewable Energy: Discover the Fuel of the Future with 20 Projects*. White River Junction, VT: Nomad Press, 2016.

Steele, Philip. *Analyzing Climate Change: Asking Questions, Evaluating Evidence, and Designing Solutions*. New York, NY: Cavendish Square, 2019.

Thomas, Keltie. *Rising Seas: Flooding, Climate Change and Our New World*. Richmond Hill, ON: Firefly Books, 2018.

Websites

Read about the consequences of climate change at:

www.climatekids.nasa.gov/climate-change-evidence

Find out more about climate change at:

www.c2es.org/content/climate-basics-for-kids

The U.S. Energy Information Administration (EIA) has useful information on renewable energy sources at:

www.eia.gov/kids

Discover more about Zero Waste at:

www.zerowasteusa.org

Publisher's note to educators and parents:
Our editors have carefully reviewed these websites to ensure that they are suitable for students. Many websites change frequently, however, and we cannot guarantee that a site's future contents will continue to meet our high standards of quality and educational value. Be advised that students should be closely supervised whenever they access the Internet.

Index